A CENTURY OF BENTHAM

Compiled by

David Johnson

LANDY PUBLISHING
1998

© Copyright is claimed by David Johnson and by Landy Publishing.

British Library Cataloguing in Publication Data.
A catalogue record for this book is available from the British Library.

ISBN 1 872895 40 9

Printed by Nayler The Printer Ltd., Accrington. Tel: 01254 234247

Landy Publishing have also published:

Bygone Bentham by Joseph Carr
A Lancashire Look by Benita Moore
Lancashire, this, that an' t'other by Doris Snape
Threads of Lancashire Life by Winnie Bridges

A catalogue of available publications may be had from:
Landy Publishing
'Acorns', 3 Staining Rise, Staining, Blackpool, FY3 0BU
Tel/Fax: 01253 895678

Cover: A milkman, Richard Butterfield of Bank Head, with his children Dick and Tom Butterfield taken in 1907. The quart, pint and gill measures hang from the frame of his cart. (Photo: M. Butterfield)

INTRODUCTION

My mother always wondered why I enjoyed having my hair cut! I should explain: I lived in Milnthorpe, and situated near the square was Harold Whitely's Barber's Shop. The room was dark, long and narrow with a bench down one side covered with magazines, and among them were copies of *Picture Post*. This magazine was fascinating and stimulated my first interest in photography. When I went to College and University, I developed an appreciation of local history. Later it seemed logical to combine these two pastimes and start to make a photographic record of Bentham.

The first book '*Bentham In Times Past*', which Peter Bolton and I produced in 1983, arose through our work at High Bentham C.P. School. My new book is a response to the many requests for something similar.

At first I was sceptical about finding new material but three months later I was overwhelmed both by the sheer volume available and the kindness and trust demonstrated by people in both High and Low Bentham in allowing me to use their treasured photographs. I have acknowledged the ownership of each picture but it is worth pointing out that certain photographs, the flood at Low Bentham is just one example, are in the possession of many people. In addition I would like to thank Mrs. J. Cardus, Mr. E. Wrathall, Mr. J. Robinson, Mr. E. Guilliam, Mr. K. Jelley, Mrs. A. Hogg, Mrs. J. Capstick, Mr. W. J. Thornton, Mrs. M. Parker, Mr. D. Bruce, Miss R. Coates, Mr. B. Williams, Mr. E. Brown, Mrs. D. Pidgeon, Mrs. M. Green-Hughes, Mr. S. Wilkinson, Mr. T. B. Marshall, Mr. P. A. Marshall and my wife Judith for their help and support in checking text and verifying various facts. I also wish to thank High Bentham C.P. School for allowing me to use and copy certain documents in their possession.

Sometimes discovering photographs was very exciting, almost like discovering buried treasure, and I felt it was a privilege to capture some of the magic of the past. By my copying them, their survival will be ensured for generations to come. It is also my hope that the local Primary Schools will be able to use this publication to generate funds for themselves.

I hope you enjoy the book and trust it will be a valuable source of information to others who wish to make deeper investigations into our heritage. The title, '*A Century of Bentham*', refers not only to the timespan covered by the material but also the 100 pictures included for your consideration and enjoyment.

David Johnson
April 1998

Aerial View of High Bentham, looking North in about 1925. This picture is the earliest view of its kind. Land was sold to build Grassrigg on 22nd December 1922 and when the photograph was taken it still stands apart. The land above it was given over to allotments. Robin Lane is mostly devoid of development. There have been three gas-holders on the site near the Angus factory. Two appear on this picture. Notice also the railway sidings at Angus' and the water tower for the steam engines in the immediate foreground.
(*Photo: B. Williams*).

BENTHAM GAS COMPANY, LIMITED.

No............   18.........

Mr. C. K. & Jones

To THE BENTHAM GAS COMPANY, LIMITED, **Dr.**

FOR GAS.

DATE.	METER INDEX.	GAS CONSUMED In Hundreds of Feet.	Price per Thousand Feet.	AMOUNT.		
				£	s.	d.
Decr 189	68600	8800	5	2	4	0
To Nov 1894	77400					
For Meter Rent					2	0
			£	2	6	0

Aerial View of High Bentham, looking West, 1952.
(*Photo: School Collection*)

Aerial View of High Bentham, looking East, in about 1955. Taken at the moment a steam train pulls away from Bentham Station this picture clearly shows the Wenning Silk Mills complex and the old bridge with the weir. Opposite is Hillcroft with its barns and stables which were built on the site of the tennis courts at the end of the recreation ground.
(*Photo: W. J. Thornton*).

Aerial View of High Bentham, looking North West, Spring 1966. Taken at the time that the first bungalow was being constructed on Furness Drive. This is a picture of a Bentham familiar to most of us today.
(*Photo: B. Williams*)

5

Town End in about 1910. The Horse and Farrier is on the right and Scotland Row (Bedlam, demolished in 1913) is just visible on the left.
(*Photo: B. Williams*)

MARK SMITH,
Horse and Farrier Inn.
+⊱ WINES AND SPIRITS. ⊰+
GOOD ACCOMMODATION FOR CYCLISTS.

Robin Lane in about 1920. Notice the fine trees and hedges.
(*Photo: S. Willkinson*)

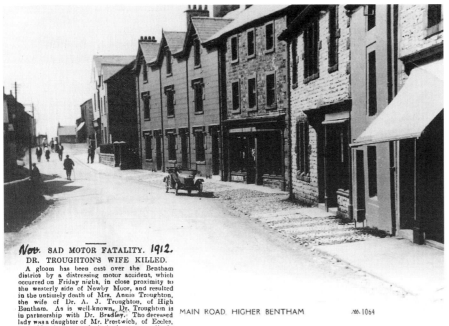

MAIN ROAD, HIGHER BENTHAM   ⋀⋀ 1064

A summers day in about 1910. The lone car probably belonged to Dr. Arthur James Troughton. He was one of the first people to own a car in Bentham and his wife was almost certainly the first person in Bentham to die in a motor car accident when he swerved and hit a tree near Butts Farm in November 1912.
(*Photo: B. Williams*)

Main Street in about 1895. Although the features on the left are familiar, the right hand side of the road, on the site occupied by the Spar, is almost unrecognisable but the house 'Farmstead' has remained almost unchanged.
(*Photo: School Collection*)

Nov. SAD MOTOR FATALITY. *1912.*

DR. TROUGHTON'S WIFE KILLED.

A gloom has been cast over the Bentham district by a distressing motor accident, which occurred on Friday night, in close proximity to the westerly side of Newby Moor, and resulted in the untimely death of Mrs. Annie Troughton, the wife of Dr. A. J. Troughton, of High Bentham. As is well-known, Dr. Troughton is in partnership with Dr. Bradley. The deceased lady was a daughter of Mr. Prestwich, of Eccles, near Manchester, and had been exceedingly popular with all classes in Bentham. Recently it had been her pleasure to accompany her husband on some of his longer journeys. On Friday night, Dr. Troughton visited, on behalf of a colleague, a patient at Newby, his wife bearing him company in their motor-car. They were returning home about ten o'clock, in the moonlight, and crossed the Moor safely, and reached the road near Butts Farm. Dr. Troughton remarked to his wife "Now we shall have a nice run into Bentham." About 300 yards from the Moor, some horses, which had strayed from the Moor and were sheltering under the hedges, suddenly dashed across the road from both sides and obstructed the car. Two of the horses were struck, and in trying to avoid serious injury the doctor swerved the car up the bank into the hedge, and it overturned. Both were thrown out, Mrs. Troughton unfortunately falling with her head on to a large stone. Dr. Troughton fell on the grass and escaped with a shaking. His first thought was naturally for his wife. He did not fear the worst for sometime as she was able to talk. He laid her on the motor rugs, and proceeded to Mr. Parker's, Butts Farm, for assistance. Returning to his wife he helped her a portion of the way to the farm, and then Mr. Parker came up and helped him. The injured lady remained at the farm till midnight, by which time a cab arrived to convey her to her home in Station-road, Bentham. Dr. Bradley was in readiness to attend to her, and diagnosed that she had sustained a fracture of the base and side of the skull. Mrs. Troughton had then relapsed into unconsciousness. Dr. Barling, of Lancaster, was summoned to perform the operation of trepanning, and was assisted by Drs. Dean and Bingham. They arrived about 4 a.m., but their efforts were beyond avail, the hemorrhage which followed the fracture causing death at noon on Saturday. Mrs. Troughton was an ardent Church worker, and was always ready to help in a good cause. Much sympathy has been expressed for Dr. Troughton and his family in their great affliction.

Main Street Bentham nº 4.

Winn's Ironmongers in about 1946. (*Photo: M. Butterfield*).

JOSHUA WINN,

Ironmonger & Oil Merchant,

Main Street, Bentham.

Any make of Mowers, Reapers & all Agricultural Implements supplied.

Wire Netting, "Ideal" and "Invincible" Fencing, Black & Galvanised Barb Wire, Fencing Wire, Galvanised Corrugated Sheets, Roofing Felts.

Agent for Jones's & Bradbury's Sewing Machines, B.S.A., Bradbury, Royal Enfield, Raleigh & Rudge Cycles & Motor Cycles.

Mangles and Washers.

Leather & Fibre Suit Cases & Attache Cases.

Market Day in about 1935. (*Photo: School Collection*)

ROYAL OAK HOTEL,
BENTHAM.

Telephone No. 4.

FAMILY & COMMERCIAL HOTEL.

First-Class Accommodation for Cyclists and Tourists.

GOOD GARAGE.

ELEANOR THWAITE, Proprietress.

Mrs. Bullock,
Tobacconist and Stationer,
Main Street, BENTHAM.

Picture Post Cards a speciality.

A choice selection of Local and other Views always in stock.

Before starting on your morning's Walk, call at BULLOCK'S
for a supply of Cigars, Cigarettes, and Tobacco for the day,
and a copy of "Walks Round Bentham." She can also supply
you with a good Country Walking Stick, or Umbrella cheap.
Umbrellas Re-Covered and Repaired.

C. KNOWLES & SONS,

Tea Merchants,

Grocers and Provision Dealers,

Kings Arms Buildings, **BENTHAM.**

Special Blends of Tea,
AND COFFEE.

Extensive Department in

Glass, China and Earthenware Goods.

Established upwards of 80 years.

The Knowles Family was in business in Bentham from 1853 and traded at the Kings Arms buildings from 1866. It is said that Mr. Rice, the owner of Grove Hill and a non conformist bought the Kings Arms Hotel to reduce the number of drinking houses in the town and was pleased to lease it to the family as a shop. The Knowles family were successful business men and developed a good grocery business. The photo of the shop was probably taken in the 1930s. The window display was photographed on 17th May 1929 to mark the occasion of the business winning a competition for a window display for Heinz products. Eventually the business closed and the Midland Bank moved into the premises in 1969. (*Photo: M. Butterfield*)

Jas. Foster,
(W. D. FOSTER,)

GROCER & CONFECTIONER

Main Street, BENTHAM.

Noted for
Home-made Bread, Scones, Teacakes & Pastry
fresh daily.

SPECIALITIES:

Slab Cake, Fruit, Madeira, Seed & Sandwich
Cakes.

Provision Department.

Farmer's Fresh Butter & Eggs.
English and Foreign Hams.
Best English and Irish Roll Bacon.
Local made Cheese.

G. W. GARLICK,

Tailor, Draper, and
Wholesale Warehouseman,

BENTHAM.

Ladies' Jackets, Coats, Capes, Raincloaks, Macintoshes,
Shawls, Corsets, Skirts, Blouses, Fur Boas, Muffs, Ties,
Laces, Gloves, Umbrellas.

HOSIERY and UNDERCLOTHING

Wolsey, Dr. Jaegars, and other good makes.

Dress Goods.

A large assortment of English and French Dress
Materials, Silks, Satins, Velvets, Blouse Materials,
Prints, Ginghams, Sateens, &c.

Men's & Boys' Ready-made Clothing.

Suits, Trousers, Overcoats, Rugs, Macintoshes,
Leggings, Umbrellas, Hats, Caps, Shirts, Pants,
and all kinds of Underclothing.

SUITINGS.   TROUSERINGS.   OVERCOATINGS.

High-class TAILORING at reasonable prices

Flannels, Shirtings, Blankets, Sheets, Counterpanes,
Ticking, Beds, Bedsteads, Mattresses.
HOUSEHOLD LINENS of every description.
Oilcloths, Linoleums, Mattings, Carpet Squares,
Art Serges, Plushes, Curtains, New Tapestries, &c.

Main Street and Garlick's Shop in about 1925.
(*Photo: E. Wrathall*)

Lairgill, in about 1900. The houses were built in the early Nineteenth Century and were once used to weave sails and other cloth on four looms installed in the basement of each of the houses. (*Photo: B. Williams*)

Mrs. SANDERSON,
Milliner, Dressmaker and Drapery Establishment,
Market Place, BENTHAM.

LADIES' MANTLES, JACKETS, and DRESS GOODS.
Newest Fancy Work in stock; also Needlecraft.

Briggs' Transfers, Crewel Silks, Canvas, Embroidery Cottons, &c., in stock

THOS. CALVERLEY,
WHOLESALE and RETAIL
Coal, Lime & Manure Merchant
BENTHAM STATION.

SILKSTONE HARDS, CARLTON HARDS,
HOUSE NUTS.   FIREWOOD.

Thomas' Phosphate Powder, Basic Slag,
Bones and Manures.

LIME for Building & Agricultural purposes.
ORDERS PROMPTLY ATTENDED TO.

Mrs. PARRINGTON,
Boot and Shoe Manufacturer,
Market Place, BENTHAM.

STRONG BOOTS made to measure—a speciality. REPAIRS of every description neatly and quickly done on the premises by experienced
workmen.

An extensive stock of Boots, Shoes, Slippers, Leggings, &c., and every
requisite connected with the trade, always on hand.

THEODORE PUMPHREY,
(LATE BRYAN HOLMES).
Main Street, BENTHAM.

Pharmaceutical Chemist,
(from Allen & Hanbury, London).
Prescriptions carefully dispensed with pure drugs.

Photographic Dealer.
All KODAK supplies.
Developing and Printing, 48 hour service.
Enlargements from your own negatives.
Dark Room on premises for convenience of
customers.

Family Grocer.
Everything for a Pic-nic.
Vacum Flasks, Lemonade Powders, Fruit-
arian Cakes, Sailor Savouries, Biscuits,
Chocolate, Nuts.

Boot & Shoe Factor.
Shooting, Fishing, Walking, Tennis, & Golf.
Agent for "K," NIL SIMILE, MASCOT,
MOCCASIN.
Repairs neatly and quickly executed.

Market Day, as viewed from Mount Pleasant, in about 1920. (*Photo: J. Cardus*)

The Brown Cow Yard. Wilson Howson was a farrier and blacksmith who used property behind the Brown Cow. The photographs on page 15 show the processes involved in putting a rim on a wheel. Shown in the photograph above are two men with a horse and cart. The man in the striped apron is thought to be 'Butcher Brownsord'. He worked at the building in the background which was Charles Metcalfe's slaughter house. Mrs. Howson owned the bakery which is now known as the Beehive. She had a piggery on the same site. The pictures were probably taken in the 1920s.
(*Photo: S. Wilkinson*)

High Bentham, _____ 187 8

Mr John Hutchinson

To ANTHONY HOWSON, Jr.,

BLACK AND WHITESMITH.

Spades, Shovels, and Forks, in great variety, always on hand.

Oct 29	8 new shoes	7	0
No 20	4 removed conveyance plates & dies	3	10
Dec 5	horse sharped 28 2 horses shp	4	6
Feb 3	2 removed	1	0
11	4 new shoes wheel greased	4	6
May 2	2 new shoes	1	9
	Settled A Howson Feb 24th 1881	2	7

CHARLES METCALFE

Brown Cow Yard,
BENTHAM.

Family Butcher, Home Killed

FRESH MEAT DAILY.

Pickled Tongue & Beef, Sausage and Brawn
a speciality.

The Cattle Auction. Richard Turner is the Auctioneer. Wendy Joel, now Wendy Heigh, stands next to him.
(*Photo: R. Turner*)

Healthy
Udders
Make
Good Cows !

With the Compliments of
The Mamasol Co. Ltd.,
Park Road, Wigan, Lancs.

Haymaking. This fine rural portrait shows Roland Dodgson and his family loading hay in a field at Townhead in about 1912. The small child in the foreground is James Dodgson.
(*Photo: M. Dodgson*)

Mewith Head Hall is one of the finest ancient buildings in Bentham. It was possibly a monastery at some point in its history. The picture was taken in about 1930 and shows Rushinder Towler drawing water from the spring.
(*Photo: B. Williams*)

The Fern Nursery, Townhead, Low Bentham, now Tom Guy's house. Bolton's not only dealt in ferns, which were popular in the Victorian era, but in a wide range of shrubs and trees. A story says that Mr. Bolton's wife left him when he insisted on keeping pigs in the house!
(*Photo: M. Dodgson*)

The Old Post Office Building.

The Post Office was once in Station Road in the house adjoining the Old Midland Bank Building (now Woods', the accountants) before moving into the Main Street (see inset). It moved across the road to its present location in the early part of this century. It incorporated the local telephone exchange and had the unique facility of a public telephone kiosk.

The photograph taken in December 1926 shows Mr. Higham (the Postmaster) with his staff. They are:-

Back Row (left to right):- John Sugden, James Lamb, B. Hutchinson, H. Stanley.

Front Row (left to right):- **David Hutchinson, Mrs. Higham, Mr. Higham (Postmaster), Jessie Bowker (Telephonist), ...?** *Extreme front*:- **John Reid (Messenger Boy)**

(*Photos: M. Slater and B. Williams*)

POST OFFICE.

Postmistress: Miss A. Stubbs. The Post Office is open for Postal Order and Postage Stamp business from 7 a.m. to 8 p.m., and for Money Order Savings Bank, Licenses, Inland Revenue Stamps, and Telegraph business from 8 a.m. to 8 p.m. Deliveries commence at 7-30 a.m. and 8-35 p.m. Mails are despatched at 12 noon and 7 p.m. Sundays: The Office is open for Telegraph and Postage Stamp business from 8 a.m. to 10 a.m. Delivery commences at 9-45 a.m., and Mails are despatched at 6 p.m. Letters for local delivery should be posted before 7 a.m. and after that, before 3 p.m. Wall boxes cleared on week-days only. Lowgill cleared at 12 p.m. Green Smithy cleared at 1-30 p.m. Mewith Head cleared at 10-30 a.m.

Low Bentham.—Postmaster: Mr. T. Boyd. This Office is open for Postal and Telegraph Work, also Money Order and Savings Bank business on week-days from 8 a.m. to 8 p.m., and on Sundays for Telegraph and Postage Stamp business from 8 a.m. to 10 a.m. Mails arrive on week-days at 8 a.m and 4 p.m. and on Sundays at 9-45 a.m. Mails are despatched on week-days at 11-30 a.m. and 6-40 p.m., and on Sundays at 1-20 p.m.

JOHN DOWNHAM,

Post Office, Low Bentham.

FRUITS, SWEETS, ICE CREAM AND ICE DRINKS, OF ALL DESCRIPTIONS,

PARTIES SUPPLIED.

Edward B. Higham,
POST OFFICE, **BENTHAM.**

Good selection of Picture Post Cards.
Stationery of all kinds.

James Lamb with his daughter Mildred (now Mildred Slater). A very special delivery!
This picture was taken in May 1920. James Lamb was one of Kitchener's Old Contemptibles and was involved in the retreat from Mons. On his uniform he wears his medals from the Great War including the Mons Star.
(*Photo: M. Slater*)

The Brown Cow, now the Coach House, has a prominent position in the centre of the Town. The Wilkinson family were the landlords for many years and this charming group showing the family and staff at the inn was taken in about 1920. The small boy (centre) is Stanley Wilkinson.

(Photo: S. Wilkinson)

GOOD STABLING. CYCLES STORED.

Brown Cow Hotel,

BENTHAM.

Good Accommodation for Pic-nic Parties. Catering. Pony and Trap for Hire. Wines and Spirits. Choice Cigars. Terms Reasonable.

MARY WILKINSON, Proprietress.

Bentham Camp was one of the earliest holiday camps in the country. Between 1908 and 1925 a tented village, as shown on the photograph, would spring up on the banks of the Wenning at Camphole. It was the brainchild of Joe Hainsworth and was operated by the family throughout its life. The camp was segregated with the single men camping on the north bank and married couples and single ladies on the southern side. They were linked by the suspension bridge shown in the picture. Joe Hainsworth is the figure to the left of the group on the bridge.
(*Photos: S. Wilkinson, R. Hainsworth*)

Ford, Ayrton Mill played a prominent part in the life of Low Bentham for a century until 1970. The various processes at the mill were illustrated on this postcard (*Photo: E. Robinson*)

FORD, AYRTON & CO., LTD., SILK SPINNERS, BENTHAM.

The gas holder at Ford, Ayrton in about 1910. Gassing was an important process in the production of silk and this small gasholder, located on the site, provided them with gas for lighting and the gassing process. (*Photo: M. Parker*)

Delivering a boiler to Ford, Ayrton Mill in about 1900. The boiler was probably supplied by Hewitt and Kellett of Bradford.
(*Photo: E. Robinson*)

Staff in the preparing room at the silk mill, 1937. Mr. D. Bruce stands on the right of the picture and his father William Bruce can be seen on the left. William Bruce was born in 1879 and worked at the mill from the age 10. He was interviewed by Dr. Dowell and recorded his recollections about the mill and the village for posterity.
The following people are on the picture (*left to right*):- Mrs. Crossen, Doris Oversby, William Bruce, Annie Jackson, Debra Braithwaite, Maisie Parker, Mary Parker, Mamie Bateson, Kathleen Bruce, Nellie Braithwaite, Douglas Bruce.
(*Photo: M. Parker*)

Silk Mill Staff 1939. There was one representative from every room in the mill. the workers are:-
Back row (left to right): Chrissie Easterby, Grace Parker, Phillis Armstrong, Mary Parker, Kathy Fry, Mary Frankland.
Front Row: Lissie Burrow, Jane Alice Parker, Nellie Townson, Edith Croft, Annie Leak.
(*Photo: M. Parker*)

Ford Ayrton staff in 1939 with Charles Ford. It is, perhaps significant that when seen in its full version this picture is signed, "*with our appreciation and good wishes R. Charles Ford, Helen B. Ford*". This small act indicates the concern and care exercised by the Ford's for the workforce. Most people recognise them as good, considerate employers who were prepared to embrace progressive ideas. The staff were:-

Front Row (left to right): Betty Marriot, Nancy Slinger, Ellen Braithwaite, Doris Robinson, Nellie Hodgson, Olive Burrow, Margaret Barker, Margaret Ewbank, Margaret Holgate, Bessie Towler, Joan Parker, Margaret Parker, Gladys Marshall, May Maunders, Margaret Burrow, Kathy Fry, Doris Foster, Lizzie Burrow, Mamie Bateson, Mary Parker.

Second Row: Army Thornborough, Bill Norcross, Albert Wilcock, Tommy Bibby, Sam Bruce, Alec Wilcock, Bob Marshall, Bill Bruce, Gervaise Ford, Charles Ford, Mr. Forrester, Herbert Ramskill, Tommy Bownass, Bill Townsend, Tom Burrow, Jim Brayshaw, Alec Smith, Joe Lockwood, Jack Carter, Joe Parker.

Third Row: Mary Atkinson, Edie Croft, Alice Lockwood, Doris Oversby, Mrs. Crosson, Maisie Parker, Sally Marshall, Alice Coates, Hope Fleming, Nellie Braithwaite, Clara Parker, Kathy Townson, Grace Parker, Chrissie Easterby, Maggie Blondell, Jannie Townson, Jessie Miller, Janet Miller, Margaret Wilson, Miss N. Townson, Miss M.J. Townson, Bessie Bateson.

Fourth Row: Lizzie Cross, Annie Jackson, Anne Herbert, Lizzie Colclough, Marion Robinson, Muriel Ramskill, Mary Fletcher, Annie Leak, Alice Brownsword, Alice Atkinson, Maud Stavely, Mary Coates, Maggie Carter, Polly Carter, Bella Carter, Elsie Burrow, Lizzie Prince, Alice Townley, Lucy Parker, Jane Alice Parker, Sarah Lockwood, Debra Braithwaite.

Fifth Row: Jim Guy, Sarah Jackson, Mary Lockwood, Mabel Brown, Audrey Hasrrison, George Lister, Jack Thwaite, Arthur Jennings, Tommy Thwaite, Dickie Braithwaite, Marjorie Wilcock, Martha Downham, Philis Armstrong, Ethel Watkinson, Albert Townley, Jack Townson, Jim Hosfield, John Burrow, Jim Miller, Elsie Robinson.

Sixth Row: Bill Park, Lit Lockwood, Ben Coates, Eddie Downham, Isaac Oldfield, Billy Noble, Dougie Bruce, John Wilson, Hevison Bell , Bob Downham, Harold Brown, Albert Burrow, Ronnie Tomlinson, Arnold Robinson, Ted Burrow, Cyril Harrison, Jim Barker, Jack Walling. (*Photo: M. Moss*)

Ford, Ayrton staff with Frank Ford in 1969. Sadly changes in fashion and severe competition from the Far East forced the closure of the mill in 1970. The workers in this picture are:- *Front Row (left to right):* Susan Preston, Norma Attchison, Shirley Gregory, …?, Alice Soar, Elaine McKay, Jackie Hind, Margaret Taylor, Jean Hodgson.
Second Row: Edna Parnell, Nelly Procter, Mrs. Bullen, Ted Fairhurst, M. Smith, Frank Ford, Mr. Hawkins, Joan Parker, Marjorie Dodgson, Doris Bell, Sarah Rowe.
Third Row: May Oldfield, Cissie Wilson, Maggie Moss, Joyce Crompton, Vera Hall, Marjorie Jennings, Mary Redhead, Maureen Magooligan, Lizzie Burrow, Audrey Lister, Clara Whitford, Mrs. Bateson, Marion Robinson, Margaret Tomlinson, Marlene Close, Margaret Bruce, Joan Thistlethwaite, …? Preston, Maisie Parker.
Fourth Row: Jim Hosfield, Armistead Thornber, Ronnie Tomlinson, Bill Slee, Kenneth Smith, Raymond Redhead, Alwyn Robertshaw, Joe Lawson, Keith Brayshaw, …?, Edgar Brennand, Eddie Murray, …? *(Photo: M. Parker)*

A millrace had been in use before Ford, Ayrton's time and therefore it is difficult to know what is going on here. It is likely that the bridge is undergoing some sort of overhaul. The picture was probably taken in about 1910. Mrs. Webb the wife of a Headmaster at Bentham Grammar School used to give pupils swimming lessons in '*the cut*' or millrace as it crossed the field from the river. *(Photo D. Bruce)*

Wenning Silks in the 1930s. The remains of the original High Mill stand centrally in the mid-distance. Founded in 1750 the mill worked in tandem with the Low Mill at Low Bentham which was built 35 years later. The mills first spun wet yarn but later changed to a dry spun yarn. They survived a spate of fires during the mid-nineteenth century. At various times they were involved in the production of cotton, flax, natural and artificial silk. The site at High Bentham was extensive, stretching from near the road as far as the Bleach Works (where the Riverside Caravan Park is situated today). Conditions at the Bleach Works were horrendous with men standing barefoot in stream water, winter and summer. Many people were crippled for life. Later, when conditions allowed, the linen was bleached in the fields by stretching it on tenterhooks in the fields below Low Bottom Farm on the other side of the river. The process gradually became more mechanised and 'humane' but eventually the works closed in 1903. A polish factory existed for a while on the same site. (*Photo: W. J. Thornton*)

Wenning Silks in about 1933. The High Mill became known as Wenning Mills Limited in 1915 but this venture closed in 1926. In 1927 the business was bought by Scottish Artificial Silks Limited and by 1931 Wenning Silks Ltd. had taken possession of the mill. It was owned by the Kattan family who wove artificial silk. Incidentally the fields in the foreground were some of those used in the bleaching process.
(Photo W. J. Thornton)

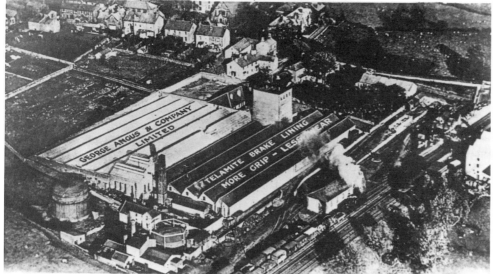

GEORGE ANGUS & Co. LTD

Office –
Johns Works
castle-upon-Tyne.

Bentham Mills,
Bentham,   Lancaster.

Established
1790

'Texcela Belting increases production."

George Angus & Co. Ltd. owes its existence to a chance discovery by George Phillipson of Bentham who was involved in the production of silk purses. He devised an eight treadle loom which produced a woven tube. This was adapted by Robert Waithman, the mill owner, who began to weave flax hosepipes at the Low Mill. This was eventually moved to the High Mill which closed early this century. The process was then purchased by George Angus and Company from Newcastle. They used the bleach works premises temporarily until the new factory was built on the present site. By the 1920s the Company was producing Telemite brake linings and clutch plates. This photograph was part of the publicity for their product based on an aerial photograph. (*Photo: B. Williams*)

A Circular Loom, Billy Smith, foreman, in the circular weaving shed at George Angus. (*Photo: B. Williams*)

31

George Angus & Co. Ltd. For many years the factory produced belts for driving machinery but eventually hosepipe production became a major feature of work in Bentham. This photograph shows hosepipes being tested for a Royal Navy order.
(*Photo: B. Williams*)

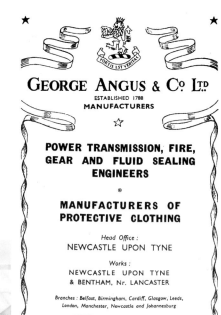

GEORGE ANGUS & Cº Lᵀᴰ

ESTABLISHED 1788
MANUFACTURERS

☆

POWER TRANSMISSION, FIRE, GEAR AND FLUID SEALING ENGINEERS

●

MANUFACTURERS OF PROTECTIVE CLOTHING

Head Office :
NEWCASTLE UPON TYNE

Works :
NEWCASTLE UPON TYNE
& BENTHAM, Nr. LANCASTER

Branches : Belfast, Birmingham, Cardiff, Glasgow, Leeds,
London, Manchester, Newcastle and Johannesburg

Agents throughout the World

George Angus & Co. Ltd., showing the factory, railway sidings, cattle pens and part of the Parish Hall or the '*Tin Tabernacle*' (extreme right). The Parish Hall played a key roll in village life. It was used for dances (to the accompaniment of Parker's Band), amateur dramatics, Gilbert and Sullivan productions and many events which added to the quality of communal life.

(*Photo: B. Williams*)

Low Bentham Gala Day has been a feature of village life for many years. This scene, recorded in about 1960, shows contestants for the Fancy Dress Competition on the field near Bridge House.
(*Photo: M. Parker*)

High Bentham had its Gala day too. This picture is taken in the small field at the western end of the Recreation Ground in the late 1930s and shows everyone gathering for the gala tea. (*Photo: W. J. Thornton*)

A garden party at High Bentham in about 1957 was held in the field opposite Angus' where the Tennis Courts were located. The photograph shows Reg. Suart trying his luck at a side show. (*Photo: Johnson Collection*)

Bentham Novelty Band was formed from local talent, mostly from Low Bentham. They performed at many local events, including galas, in the 1930s. They are:-

Back Row (left to right): Mr. Prince, Tim Houldsworth, Jim Miller, Stan Ellershaw, Isaac Oldfield, ...?, ...?, Tom Hodgson, Jim Townson, ...?, Bert Maunders, Ben Coates, ...?, Jack Walling, Frank Coates, Percy Wilcock, Bill Holmes.

Front Row: Albert Coates, Harry Coates, Arthur Jennings, Eddie Downham, Tommy Bibby, Jack Burrow, John Burrow, Jack Horton.

(*Photo: M. Parker*)

Nellie Luke's Dancing Class was a feature of village life during the 1940s and '50s. They presented shows for many different occasions. This photograph shows the dancing troupe performing in the Town Hall in about 1940.

They are (*left to right*):- Audrey Thompson, Dorothy Brammer, Rene Titterington, Margaret Carr, Marjorie Ammatt, ...?, Shirley Chamberlain, Winnie Robinson, Grace Jenkinson, Edna Lister.

(*Photo: C. Jennings*)

Tea Time. An annual feature of village life was the Children's Christmas Party. This photograph was taken in the 1960s at the Parochial School and shows the helpers taking a welcome break while the children were being entertained. One can clearly distinguish the following in the photograph:-

Back Row (left to right): John Brass, Harold Lister, Jack Lister, Edwin Coates.

Middle Row (Left to right) Hilda Lister, Edna Burrow, Hilda Coates, Faith Wilson, Ruby Pridmore and Cissy Wilson.

Front Row (left to right): Rhoda Coates, Mary Burrow, Jenny Wheildon, Mary Parker and Amy Wilson.

(Photo: M. Parker)

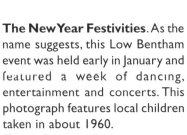

The New Year Festivities. As the name suggests, this Low Bentham event was held early in January and featured a week of dancing, entertainment and concerts. This photograph features local children taken in about 1960.

(Photo: C. Jennings)

The Cross at Low Bentham was constructed in 1902 to mark the Coronation of Edward VII. It was a community project designed and promoted by the Rector, the Revd. Percy Coates. The picture is one of a pair taken of the event. It shows the villagers gathered at the site prior to the laying of the foundations. Mr. Willan from Greenfoot Farm was made Constable of The Cross. At the official opening, conducted by Richard Wilcock, the Rector distributed Coronation mugs to the children.
(*Photo: Tom Guy*)

Cafe: STONE GATE HOUSE,

Interesting Old Residence, (1579)

Board Residence
or Apartments.
Bracing Air.
Delightfully Situated
Fishing.
2 acres beautiful Grounds
Accom, Motors.
Home Produce.
Tea Gardens.
Parties Catered for.
Pony Cart for Hire.

Proprietors :

Mr. & Mrs. WALTER HAINSWORTH,
Low Bentham,
Nr. Lancaster.

(Late Morecambe Holiday Camp).

Stonegate House, Low Bentham. In Bibby's Book '*A History of Bentham*' it is stated that Stonegate house is believed to be the oldest house in Bentham. It is thought that this photograph features a celebration held to mark Empire Day in 1911. The event featured floats from different parts of the Empire. This may explain why the Australian Flag is flying above the Institute!

(*Photo: M. Parker*)

Settle Rural District Council Road Maintenance Gang Steam Roller parked across the lane leading to Pye's Corn Mill. The wonderful character with the beard, in front of the name plate, is the late Evelyn Willan's father. The picture was probably taken in about 1935.

(Photo: Tom Guy)

The Old Bridge showing the weir, St. Margaret's Church and 'The Wenning'.
(*Photo: R. Turner*)

The Old Bridge and Weir, a fish's eye-view!
(*Photo: W. J. Thornton*)

The River Wenning and the bathing hut from the old bridge. The weir ensured a head of water to the High Mill. From a millrace near the bridge water flowed in a culvert under the mill and back into the Wenning near the Bleach Works. This arrangement created a natural pool above the bridge. It was used by the locals as a bathing pool and the photograph shows the hut which belonged to Bentham Amateur Swimming Club. (*Photo: E.K. Duesbury*)

The Flood of 13th December 1964 swept part of the old bridge away at 7.10 am. This photograph shows the bridge shortly after it was destroyed. Note Hillcroft, with some of the Council houses completed in the background. This catastrophe was caused by a deterioration in the condition of the weir which ultimately collapsed. A Bailey bridge was erected from the site of the old bathing hut to a point on Richard Turner's side. Rebuilding commenced on 2nd May 1966 and the new bridge was officially opened on 5th May 1968 (*Photo: S. Wilkinson*)

The River Wenning has been a source of beauty and relaxation for generations. Ramblers are all familiar with Shaky Bridge. A glance at the river bed reveals the existence of foundations of several bridges. These pictures show two predecessors of the present bridge. The earlier, sturdier structure (top) was probably photographed in about 1915 whereas the lower photograph appears to have been taken in the late 1920s. (*Photos: B. Williams and S. Wilkinson*)

St. Margaret's Church was built in 1837 by Hornby Roughsedge, the owner of Bentham Mill and the occupant of Bentham House. It became a separate ecclesiastical parish in 1872. This group picture, taken in about 1940, shows the Revd. W.F. Harden (*centre*) and St. Margaret's Church Choir. The man in the dark suit sitting to the left of Revd. Harden is Mr. G. P. Gill, the organist and headteacher of Bentham Grammar School. The view of the church entrance and drive shows Elizabeth Wilkinson standing in front of the rather unusual, massively constructed, church gates. (*Photos: C. Jennings and S. Wilkinson*)

The Parish Church of St. John The Baptist, Low Bentham, is believed to date back to Saxon times. It was the principal church for this part of Ewecross. Until the middle of the nineteenth century the Parish covered a vast area from Chapel Le Dale to Bentham. The building in the picture is the forerunner of today's building. It was built in 1822 and demolished in 1876 making this photograph at least 122 years old!
(*Photo: R. Coates*)

Men's and Women's Bible Classes were only one part of the religious and social activities centering on the church. There were many other organisations such as snooker and bowling clubs, choirs and musical groups which made it an important focus for village life. (*Photos: T. Guy and C. Jennings*)

St. Boniface's Roman Catholic Church was built in 1866 on the site of a brewery. The new church was consecrated in 1960. The photograph shows the chancel and altar in the 1930s.
(*Photo: S. Pridmore*)

Winters are often mild in this area and our children view snow as a treat (as do some adults!). The winters of 1939 and 1940 had their moments as these pictures reveal! The pictures were taken in 1939 and show the Wenning near Ford Ayrton's and Burton Road beyond Townhead. Miss Clark, the Headteacher at High Bentham C.P. School, wrote "...*during Saturday and Sunday 27th and 28th there was the worst snow storm known for years. The terrific winds blew drifts of 10 feet high. The roads were impassable so that only 30 children could get to school.*"
(*Photos: Bernard Williams and Christine Jennings*)

These two snow pictures were taken at the top of Robin Lane on 31st January 1940. They clearly show the size of the drifts which had quickly accumulated to block the road.
(*Photos: M. Butterfield*)

High Bentham Football Club
taken in about 1965. Mr. Jack Park can
be seen standing on the extreme right.
(*Photo: J. Cardus*)

Low Bentham Football Club in about 1955. *Children* (*left to right*) Brian Smith, Keith Parker, Terry Hodgson, Alan Parker, Valerie Wilcock. *Front Row Adults*: Grace Parker, …? Smith, Billy Noble, Cyril Tomlinson, Gordon Noble, Lionel Titterington, Bud Cross. *Second Row*: Joyce Halstead, Hetty Slee, Betty Dodgson, Harry Lang, Ken Houldsworth, Paul Magooligan, …?, Colin Wilcock, Jim Houldsworth, Charlie Bell, Eric Guy. *Amongst the back row*: Frank Dodgson, Thomas Burrow, Edward Bibby, John Burrow, Mary Alice Tomlinson, Armistead 'Armie' Thornber, Bill Houldsworth, Eric Maudsley, Joe Burrow. (*Photo: M. Parker*)

Low Bentham Snooker Club taken at the Rectory in in about 1920.
(*Photo: C. Jennings*)

Low Bentham Bowling Club in about 1935. The group consists of:-
Back Row (left to right): Tom Bownass, William Davidson, William Walling, Jack Burrow, Ben Coates, Mr. Gregson, Jack Walling, Albert Coates.
Front Row: Frank Coates, Edward Holmes, T.W. Twaddle, Canon Garrad, Harry Coates, Arthur Jennings, Ben Clarkson.
(*Photo: R. Pridmore*)

'Bentham Wanderers' Low Bentham
Football Club in about 1910. High and
Low Bentham had their own teams. Low
Bentham used to play on the Punch
Bowl field.
(Photo: C. Jennings)

Low Bentham Cricket Team in
about 1910.
(Bentham Grammar School Archives)

Bentham Golf Course and Ingleborough.

The Golf Club was formed in 1922. Times have changed since the days when cows grazed the course. These photographs, taken in 1951 *(bottom right)* and 1949 pre-date the construction of the new clubhouse which was opened in 1974. We are fortunate that it has been possible to name many members. On the large 1949 group *(centre)*. They are:- *Front Row (left to right)*: Joyce Cowgill, Elizabeth Cowgill, Wendy Wilson, Nellie Bradley with her 3 children, Kendal Duesbury, Blanche Slinger with Barry Slinger in front, Michael Slinger with Keith Slinger in front, Margaret Ewbank Susan Wilson, Lena Wilson, Beth Duesbury, Hanson Carr, Bob Guy, Mr. Tyler, …?, Vera Cocking, Mary Foster. *Back Row*: Arthur Briscoe, Mrs. Briscoe, Mrs. Teague, …? Mrs. Procter, …?

MEMBER'S OPEN DAY : 10th July 1949

cont. Mrs. Blakey, Ronnie Procter, …? Milton E. Bradley, …? Mr. Bateson, Mrs. N. Thompson, Mollie Thompson, W. D. Foster, Andrew McGregor Wood, …?, W. Dewsbury, Mr. Dean, Charles Cowgill, Roy Cocking.
On the bottom right 1951 picture they are:- *Front Row (left to right)*: Mrs. Wilson, Susan Wilson, Joyce Cowgill, Vera Cocking, Mrs. McGregor Wood, Wendy Wilson, Elizabeth Cowgill, …Cocking (child), Mrs. McIntyre, Roger Booth (boy). *Back Row*: Andrew Mcgregor Wood, …? McIntyre, …McIntyre (son), Charles Cowgill, Mrs. Thompson, Mollie Thompson, Peggy Duke (with Philippa), …?, Mrs. Blakey, Bill Duesbury, Arthur Ambrose Briscoe, Beth Duesbury, David Booth, Roy Cocking, Ken Duke.
(Photos: K. Duke and M. Butterfield)

Bentham Silver Band parading through the streets at the head of a procession (possibly the Sunday School Treat) in about 1925. The band was formed in the 1860s and was not wound up until 1969. In its heyday it hosted 'The Bentham Brass Band Competition' and played an important part in town life particularly at galas, fairs and major festivals. It took part in the Brass Band championships at Belle Vue, Manchester in the 1950s.

The group photograph taken in 1946 was taken to show the band in its new livery. Mr. R.C. Ford, the owner of Ford Ayrton Silk Mill sits in the centre of the group. The photograph was taken at his residence, "Sandy Croft" on Low Bentham Road. The other members were:-

Back Row (left to right): **John Ball, Fred Jenkinson, Harry Smith, Robert Robinson, Fred Watson, Ken Watkinson, Stuart Wilkinson.**

Third Row: **Tom Watkinson, George Whitfield, Edward Robinson, Ernest Thompson, Paul Magoolagan, Jim Robinson, George Pedder, Jack Easterby, Herbert Bibby.**

Second Row: **John Whinray, Tom Bibby, Ron. Tomlinson, Jim Patterson, R.C. Ford, George Downham, Mark Brennand, Alec Ellershaw.**

Front Row: **John Houghton, Alan Wills, Francis Holmes, Neil Thompson, Ken Houlsworth.**

(Photos: M. Parker and W Thornton)

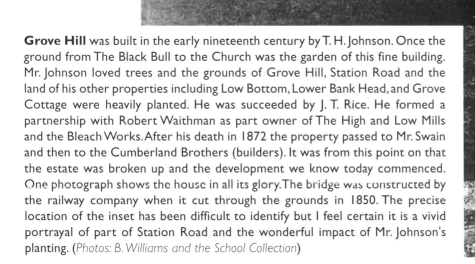

Grove Hill was built in the early nineteenth century by T. H. Johnson. Once the ground from The Black Bull to the Church was the garden of this fine building. Mr. Johnson loved trees and the grounds of Grove Hill, Station Road and the land of his other properties including Low Bottom, Lower Bank Head, and Grove Cottage were heavily planted. He was succeeded by J. T. Rice. He formed a partnership with Robert Waithman as part owner of The High and Low Mills and the Bleach Works. After his death in 1872 the property passed to Mr. Swain and then to the Cumberland Brothers (builders). It was from this point on that the estate was broken up and the development we know today commenced. One photograph shows the house in all its glory. The bridge was constructed by the railway company when it cut through the grounds in 1850. The precise location of the inset has been difficult to identify but I feel certain it is a vivid portrayal of part of Station Road and the wonderful impact of Mr. Johnson's planting. (*Photos: B. Williams and the School Collection*)

Station Road. A rural spring scene never likely to be witnessed again! It was probably in the 1930s. The tennis courts are visible on the right of the picture. Could the gentleman in the foreground be a railway employee on his way home? (*Photo: Mary Parker*)

The Cumberland Brothers' office. This was built in the grounds of Grove Hill after the firm purchased the property in the late nineteenth century. The original entrance to Grove Hill stood on the site of the office. The first floor became the quarters for the Liberal Club and the small balcony allowed access to the flag pole so that the Union Jack could be raised. (*Photo: Bernard Williams*)

LIBERAL CLUB.

Hon. President: Wm. Clough, Esq., M.P.; Vice-Presidents: Messrs. T. Benson P. Ford, Ed. Ayrton, Robt. Greenep and Thos. Wilcock. Chairman: Mr. Rd. Clapham. Vice-Chairmen: Messrs. Wm. Hutchinson and Bryan Holmes. Treasurer: Mr. Wm. Greenep. Asst. Treasurer: Mr. Robert Gorrill. Auditor: Mr. Ed. Ayrton. Secretary: Mr. Thomas Knowles. Games Secretary: Mr. Wm. Hy. Greenep. Librarians: Messrs. W. H. Greenep and Bryan Holmes. Committee: Messrs. John Thompson, J. Pickup, John C. Clapham, John Windle, John Stephenson, Edwin Jackman, Thos. Knowles, jun., and Wm. Stephenson.

Hillcroft was formerly known as Bentham House. The first resident was Charles Parker, a minister of the Society of Friends. He was also the much respected mill owner. After he moved to Yealand in about 1815 the house became the property of Hornby Roughsedge. He too was the owner of the mill and purchased the Manor of Ingleton from the Parker family of Browsholme Hall. He was responsible for building St. Margaret's Church. It is believed the church was named after his wife who was also called Margaret. He left Bentham in 1851 and died in 1859. He was buried in Grasmere Church yard. The house next passed to William Waithman. He lived there

until 1872 but after he departed it was divided into two houses. Eventually the whole house was taken by the Miss Ralph's, who renamed it Hillcroft, and turned it into a private school for girls. It was ideal for a school with beautiful grounds but it closed in 1934. For a couple of years it became another school belonging to the Parents National Educational Union before it was eventually made into flats . It was demolished in the late 1960s to make way for the small estate which stands there now.

(*Photos: B. Williams*)

The Wenning Hotel was once known as Sisson's Victoria Hotel. As the photograph taken in about 1895 reveals it was a substantial building constructed to accommodate travellers arriving by rail. It was surrounded by fine trees. Early this century it became the vicarage until 1927 when it reverted to being a hotel. It was renamed The Wenning Hotel and was run by Mr. and Mrs. Tom Townson. George Angus and Company purchased it in 1952 and converted it into office and conference accommodation.

(*Photo: B. Williams*)

A Trade Stand at an exhibition (venue not known) by Carr and Co. drapers and grocers of Low Bentham. Probably taken between 1900 and 1910.
(*Photo: M. Parker*)

"Old Folks at Home."

14

Dec 8ᵗʰ .... 1942.

Mʳˢ *T. Shrigi*

Bought of **BIRKETT STABLES**
Grocer and Corn Dealer
LOW BENTHAM, Near Lancaster
Phone No. Bentham 346   Drapery Hardware. Crockery. etc.
Home Fed Hams   Local Cheese   Farmers' Brushes a Speciality

DRINK   DELICIOUS   MAZAWATTEE   TEA.

The Co-operative Society Stores, Low Bentham was registered in Wakefield on 18ᵗʰ December 1891. It was welcomed by the villagers who had previously been forced to walk to High Bentham to use the facilities of a Co-operative Society. This picture was taken in about 1918. The stores closed in 1960 but the area is still known as Co-op corner. (*Photo: M. Parker*)

The Punch Bowl Inn was built in the eighteenth century and the barn dates from 1708. The Inn commands a strategic position at the bridge and road junction. The principal route to Lancaster used to be the road to Millhouses and then on to Wray. It was the introduction of the turnpike road with its tollgates, such as the one at Low Bentham, which heralded the arrival of improved road surfaces and the increased importance of the B6480 through Wennington.

(*Photos: Tom Guy and B. Williams*)

High Bentham C. P. School. The photograph with Robin Lane and St. Margaret's Sunday School as a background was taken in about 1930 and shows Miss Atkinson's class posing for their photograph in the lower yard. (The area where the new extension was built).

The other photograph shows Miss Park (now Mrs. Cardus) with her class in 1954. She thinks the space on the back row occurred because a child had run to the toilet!

(*Photo: J. Cardus*)

Low Bentham C.P. School. The top photograph was taken in 1955 whereas the lower picture dates from 1936. The children in this picture are:-

Back Row: Cyril Tomlinson, Gordon Noble, Fred Crossley, Jim Houldsworth, Thomas Robinson, Ted Capstick.

Fourth Row: Thomas Cornthwaite, Harold Wilson.

Third Row: Mavis Noble, Myrah Hope, Madge Fleming, Jennie Tomlinson, Joan Burrow, Audrey Bell, Helen Fleming, Thelma Noble, Mavis Wilcock, Eunice Tomlinson.

Second Row: Annie Kellet, Dorothy Wilcock, Mary Raynor, Phoebe Taylor, Norah Wilcock, Enid Capstick.

Front Row: Clifford Ellershaw, Harry McCay, Ronnie Taylor.

(*Photos: C. Jennings and T. Capstick*)

Low Bentham Parochial School 1922. The school opened in 1849 and closed 131 years later in 1980. The photograph shows the older pupils with their teacher Miss Ives.
(*Photo E. Robinson*)

Bentham Grammar School in about 1908 with the Revd. Theodore Bayley Hardy. He was Headmaster from 1907 until 1913 before moving to become the Vicar of Hutton Roof. He joined the ranks as Chaplain Hardy during the First World War and for his gallantry he was awarded the V.C., D.S.O., and M.C.

Bentham Grammar School Football Team 1913-14.
(*Photo: Bentham Grammar School Archives*)

(*Photo: Bentham Grammar School Archives*)

SURGAM

FOUNDED. 1726

Grammar School,

BENTHAM, Lancaster,

CHAIRMAN OF GOVERNORS:
REV. CANON PERCY COATES, M.A.,
Rector of Bentham; Rural Dean of Ewecross.

HEAD MASTER:
G. PERCY GILL,
1900-1914, Headmaster of "English School,"
Frankfort-on-Maine.
1914-1916, Second Master at Ruthin Public
School, N. Wales.
1916-1921, Assistant Master (Music) Giggleswick
School, Settle.

Prospectus on application.